Every Moment Is A Poem, Every Poem A Song

To Helen,

Live, Love, Dream!

Diane

8/30/17

Every Moment Is A Poem, Every Poem A Song

DIANE RIVOLI

ISBN: 1523914335
ISBN 13: 9781523914333
Library of Congress Control Number: 2016902605
CreateSpace Independent Publishing Platform
North Charleston, South Carolina

COVER ILLUSTRATION BY JOSH RIVOLI

ALSO BY DIANE RIVOLI:

License – A Novel

As always, for Joseph

Contents

Introduction

I've been writing poems all my life. My joys and my hopes, my fears and regrets, my musings and contemplations live there. I take pleasure in wrapping words around a thought or an emotion. I get lost in the cadence and the rhyme.

And I sit in wonder at how much can be said with so few words. How the emotions of a moment can be captured or an entire life can be lived. How you can be taken for a lighthearted romp, given a nostalgic kiss, or a cold, hard slap in the face.

I love the way poems sneak up on you, drawing you in with hints and subtle nuances and then suddenly swelling with intensity and meaning.

Some people do not care for poems. They have no patience for the cadence and the rhyme. They do not know how to unwrap the words and let their meaning soar.

Some poems fight back, despite the reader's attempts to understand them; because not every poem is for everyone. If a poem is for you, it will speak to you. Your insides will tingle; you'll get a catch in your throat; your eyes might get misty or light up in a smile. You do not choose the poem. The poem chooses you.

There are times when a poem speaks to you and at first you can't explain why. But your heart knows. It feels the meaning; tucked between the words or hidden behind them. It tells you to close your eyes and see with your ears, listen to the words as they roll softly on your tongue and melt into your soul. Then you will know why the poem has chosen you.

The poems that I share with you here span years. Many of them were included in my novel 'License', scattered among the chapters, adding depth and dimension to the characters and another perspective from which to experience the lives they lived.

My hope is that they will speak to you, touch you in ways large and small, show you that life is made up of moments, that every moment is a poem, and every poem a song.

1

Time likes to play tricks on us. A moment can seem to crawl along and last forever. And years can seem to pass by in a glimpse, leaving us wondering where we were looking and what we were doing as they went flying by.

'"Bye Bye, Dixie," Lainey Andrews whispered as she peaked through the curtains and watched the blue Jetta back out of the driveway and head east.

She sat on the edge of the bed and smiled. Her Dixie, off on her own. Her Dixie, she was so proud of her! Her Dixie, her brilliant, beautiful Dixie. She had been such a tiny bundle when she was born. Where had that tiny bundle gone? Suddenly she was sobbing, tears streaming down her cheeks.'

Excerpt from 'License – A Novel'

Tiny Bundle

Where did that tiny bundle go?
The one I held so tight.

The one I showered with kisses and hugs
And comforted during the night.

Is she in her highchair?
Is she in her big girl bed
With her thumb in her mouth
Clutching her blanket with the silky edge?

Is she out at the bus stop
Waiting for the bus
To take her to kindergarten
To learn letters and numbers and other important stuff?

Or perhaps she's out with her father
Learning how to drive.
Or in the bathroom shaving her legs
For the very first time.

No, no
There she is now!
Walking across the stage
In her cap and gown.

Now her car is packed full
And the house seems so empty.
She's off on her own.
"Don't forget to call me!"

Where did that tiny bundle go?
She grew into a woman.
But I still remember her sweet baby smell
And the touch of her little hand.

2

We change as we grow older – toothless grins become smiles, curiosity becomes knowledge, impetuous becomes prudent, boundless becomes measured. Naivety gets lost to experience. Daydreams, grand schemes, awe and wonder fade in the glare of maturity.

But sometimes the wide-eyed child still within us comes skipping out, somewhat hesitant and slightly tempered, to paint a fresh glow on our faded dreams.

Burnished To Golden

Once
Long ago, I was a spring fresh bud
Unfurling bright petals to the sun
I dreamed I would climb a tall mountain
And at the top
I'd raise my arms up so high
And slide
Screaming and smiling
All the way down

Time
Keeps a steady rhythm that has carried me along
Life following, in rising and falling notes
Singing an unscored song
Harmony in the repeating chorus
Unplanned changes in between
A quarter turn towards heaven or hell
Flat to sharp, sharp to flat
Playing out on the strings

Now
I am an autumn leaf
Burnished golden
And hanging emboldened
By the passing of time
I am a dolphin
Breaking the surface
And leaping joyous
Into an azure sky
Brave enough finally to seize the glory of my day
But the coming part takes way too long
And when I get there
You can't stay

Ever
The spring fresh bud
I live and breathe
I dance and sing
And I hold tight to your hand

I know that if perfection exists
It lies there

Sometimes
I still dream I'll climb that tall mountain
And at the top
I'll grip the bar till my knuckles turn white
And I'll slide
Screaming and smiling
All the way back down

3

Inspiration is everywhere. It comes to me at the least expected moments - floating on a breeze, tied up in a knot, woven in a scrap of fabric, popping from the letters on a license plate.......

GUS

I've been seeing Gus a lot lately
I'm not sure why
He pops up unexpectedly
Always a surprise
There must be something
He's trying to tell me

Gus passed by me
Near the ice cream stand
I was sitting on a bench with my cone in hand
He was glistening golden in the sun

A five minute shower
Can ruin a picnic
Clammy clothes
Soggy rolls
Pools in the paper plates
But five minutes doesn't mean a thing
To parched earth still dry and cracked
To wilting flowers still desperate for drink

Another day I saw Gus
In a grasshopper green car
Speeding down the left hand lane

Hot or cold
Pleasure or pain
Sometimes they all feel the same

On my way home from work
Two lengths ahead
I came across Gus
In sporty jokester red

What can you do
When you fluff and toot
Except giggle and laugh
And hold your breath
Batten down the hatches
Or flap the covers
And chase the vapors away

And there was Gus
In the hardware store lot
Standing crooked
And taking up two spots

Sometimes your eyes can play tricks
It's a bending of the rays
A parallactic shift
That Ferris Wheel in the distance
Summer bright and gay
Is really a tree
Winter bare and gray

One day waiting at the traffic light
I saw Gus over to the right
Slow to start
and melancholy blue

You think you're special
I think I'm special
We all think we're special
Who are we fooling?
We are never the chosen ones

In the waning light of dusk
I spotted him again
All mussed and skewed
And pushed aside
Tall weeds hovering

At his right and at his left
Looking quite abandoned
But his identity was still intact
Gus!

Any moment
The moment can change

Now I'm scared
Pain weird dreams
Disturb my sleep
My brains leak out through my ears
What am I supposed to do?
What's he trying to say?
I don't really even know him
GUS
Just three letters
Three letters on a license plate

4

One of the truest statements to be said about life is that any moment the moment can change.

A car runs a red light, a bolt of lightening strikes, a wrong slice of the knife, and the day's plans, or the course of your whole life, will never be the same.

And what might it feel like to be lying on the ground, your blood a sticky red puddle by your side?

'Always be aware of your surroundings. His father had repeated that advice to Greg many, many times. It was good advice; advice that Greg wasn't remembering now. He was busy making plans, thinking about Dixie; completely lost in thought, completely unaware.'
Excerpt from 'License – A Novel'

Brothers In Arms

The sound of his blood rushing through his veins throbbed in his ears.

He had to go get those flowers for Dixie!

He heard screams and yelling, scuffling and running, sirens. He saw flashing lights and flashing colors.

A partially flattened french fry lay inches from his face, bits of ketchup stuck to it like eyes and a nose, or like blood.

"Tough luck, Dude," it whispered to him, its little ketchup eyes mournful and hopeless. "Brothers in arms we are, brothers in arms."

He had to go see Dixie! Tell her he was sorry.

But his ears felt stuffed with cotton. His eyes would not stay focused.

He had to ask her how she was doing, ask her about her hopes and her dreams.

Everything he was seeing and hearing seemed to decompose in his mind before his brain could make sense of them.

Maybe she could hold him.

Someone had turned him over onto his back. Wads of paper were being pressed to his stomach, darkening quickly as they became soaked with blood.

Maybe she could rub his head with her cool hands.
Maybe she could stop this terrible, terrible pain.

"Stay with me now. Stay with me," they said.

5

It was one of those nights. I lay on the futon, my mind exhausted but my body restless, tossing and turning, unable to sleep.

But I must have fallen asleep at some point because...I woke up. And the dream I awoke from had been so intense and extraordinarily vivid, I had to believe that somehow, on some plane, in some alternate universe, it must have been real.

I experienced every detail - the colors, the textures, the lighting, even the smells. And days later it was still with me. This was someplace I had been. This was some life I had lived. Or maybe, some life yet to come.

Premonition?

I had a dream, an unreal dream
It was so surreal
But it was so clear
There was an apartment
Our apartment in the city
I had forgotten it was there

Solid walnut trim framing ocean blue walls
Smooth granite counter tops
In speckled creams and tans and browns
A brick kitchen floor and a gleaming oak table
Muted lighting like the setting sun through a lace curtain

Bullet holes in the window, in the wall
Leftovers from the spaghetti dinner
Still in the fridge
Is it a premonition?
Of life?
Of death?
I think my mother's waiting there
Of heaven?

The morning sun
Upon my eyes
Wakes me from my sleep
My dreams rise up like silvery smoke
Only mine to keep
For an instant?
Not this dream
This dream stayed

6

Those that study dreams say that most dreams deal with misfortune or negative emotions – frantically searching and never finding, desperate to arrive yet never arriving, running in panic down endless hallways that have no adjoining rooms and no exit sign.

They also say that some people seem to dream in color, some in black and white, and that some people don't really know one way or the other. That would be me - one of the ones that don't know.

I live the dream and feel the dream. But the color, if there is any, goes unnoticed or unremembered.

Except sometimes. Sometimes one object in my dream will scream out to be noticed. Its color explodes before my dreaming eyes, brilliant among the blacks, whites and grays. The GREEN leaves on the tree. The RED collar around the dog's neck. The PINK jacket the desperate girl wears as she runs. And runs. And runs.

'She pulled her Jetta over to the side of the road, waiting for the tears to diminish so she could see again, disgusted and angry with herself for being a spineless cry baby. And angry at herself as well, for

a long list of other transgressions that she whipped herself for every day, number one on the list being - All My Fault.'
    Excerpt from 'License – A Novel'

The Dream

She must run, she must hide
She is frantic to get away
But her jacket is bright pink
And on her feet are heavy weights forcing her to stay

Like a goose she waddles with her heavy weights
A goose with no wings to fly
Except for the bright pink jacket
Which flaps and billows by her side

They are everywhere she goes
Those from whom she tries to flee
They are in the next room
She turns her face so as not to be seen
They are around the next corner
She slips behind a person or behind a tree

Now she is standing in line
With her bright pink jacket
With the weights upon her feet
Waiting to order an ice cream cone
Cool, creamy and sweet

She anticipates the freshness
The cold melting smoothness
Her tongue is poised to lick the dulcet cream
But instead she holds a spicy burrito
Filled with salty meat and pasty refried beans

Now she is in the restroom
Her feet are bare
Nothing to protect them from what has been left
Wet and slick, tacky and smeared
On the filthy tile floor

Her mind cringes and screams
Pictures grotesque things
That will attach to her skin, absorb through her pores
Soak into her blood and into her soul

And they are there, always there
They see everything she does
She can't run, she can't escape, she can't hide
They stare at her, she stares at them
Her face reflected
In her own haunted eyes

7

Many years ago, my local newspaper ran a Valentine's Day contest calling for readers to send in stories about how they had first fallen in love. Ever the poet, I entered a poem instead.

It did not win the prize of a dozen red roses but it won honorable mention and my husband's embarrassment should any of his co-workers realize the love poem in the Valentine's Day newspaper was about him!

'And Pam found herself falling in love with Boyd all over again.'
Excerpt from 'License – A Novel'

⁓

The First Time I Fell In Love

The first time I fell in love
I was only seventeen
His hair was brown
So were his eyes
And his face was the handsomest I had ever seen

I knew that it was really love
Because I felt a flutter
In my stomach
And in my heart
The place where it really matters

The second time I fell in love
I was twenty three
His hair was brown
So were his eyes
And his face was the handsomest I had ever seen

He supported me through times of pain
And in joy he shared with me
He put up with my many moods
I knew no greater love could ever be

The third time I fell in love
I was thirty three
His hair was brown
So were his eyes
And his face was the handsomest I had ever seen

He was tender, sweet and loving
Honest, thoughtful and kind
And I was glad in times of trouble
I had never changed my mind.

Because even though the brown hair
May have changed from long to short
And some wrinkles may have been added
To that handsomest of faces
Those brown eyes still sparkle
With a shine that time cannot erase

The boy that I had fallen in love with
When I was only seventeen
Is still the man that I adore
When I am thirty three

8

"Our Honeymoon' – Lainey pulled the leather embossed album down off the shelf and began flipping the pages......

With pictures for each anniversary, the album was much more than 'Our Honeymoon'. It was a yearly chronicle of their lives together and the progression of their family. She had new pictures ready to enter into the album now, 'Honeymoon #25', their silver anniversary!'

Excerpt from 'License – A Novel'

The card said:

Happy Anniversary My Darling Joseph!

Yours Forever and Always,
Diane

The gift was this poem.

⌐

Silver

The light reflected in your eyes
A silver glint

The morning dew
A silver drop on tips of grasses bent

Virgin snow in yards of white
Glitters silvery

On your head
Silver salt mixed in with peppery

Silver gold round our fingers
To mark the special day

Then till now
Twenty-five years
Our silver anniversary

9

My husband, Joe, and I were in our twenties, barely into our 8th year of marriage and just starting our little family when we met George and Mary.

Joe had recently left one job for a different one and new co-worker George, 20 years his senior, took him under his wing. They became fast friends, hunting buddies and confidants, George bestowing his knowledge and wisdom on young Joe, the son he never had.

It wasn't long before we started getting together as couples, Joe and myself, George and Mary. It was a wonderful friendship that lasted decades. Then our dear George died of cancer, leaving us all behind.

It hit Mary hard. They'd shared a life together for over 50 years, and now he was gone and she was alone.

We visit Mary often, stopping over with pizza and wings, talking about the present and the future and reminiscing about the past. On one such visit, I spotted an old photograph Mary had on her end table of herself and George when they were in their twenties. With laughter and tears, Mary told us the story behind that photo and of the night she and George first met.

I wrote this poem for her.

Gazing Out Together

Handsome, like a movie star
He gazes from the frame
How her heart had raced
When she first laid eyes on him

He's smiling
Young, bright and alive
And she, equally bright
Stands smiling by his side

Gazing out together
The future's dazzling promise
Glistening in their eyes
She gazes in now alone
Eyes swimming with nostalgia
For the life that they had known

With tenderness and passion
A family had been born
With patience, love and teamwork
A house became a home

The music and the laughter
The sun, the snow, the rain
Scents of pine and flowers
Trust on upturned face

Rainbow threads and fabrics
Canopies of forest green
Her life had been a wonder
She would never want to change

But she can still feel
The protective circle of his arm
Around her shoulders
She can still hear
His voice call out her name
How she wishes
Just this one thing
Could have stayed the same

10

Only a few years after the death of our friend George, we lost another friend to the dreaded cancer; my husband's best friend and second hunting buddy, Mike. He had been a robust man, energetic and full of life, before the cancer claimed him at the young age of 60; dedicated to his family and friends and to keeping his Ukrainian heritage alive.

It's hard to lose those we love. They have become part of us, woven into our beings. And when they die, part of us comes unraveled, leaving a ragged emptiness inside us. We stand un-anchored, trying to make sense of the senseless, and wondering where life's essence has gone.

For A Friend

He was a friend you used to talk to
With whom you had an affinity
The state of the world
The noisy red squirrel
The buck that you glimpsed through the trees

Good times shared at the table
Breaking bread, downing cold frothy brews
Nostrovia! Mno haya lita!
Good health and a long life to you!

Births and deaths and family events
Varenyky, holubchi and borshch
Walking, talking and laughing
Autumn leaves blazing
Scouting for droppings and tracks

But the future is fragile and uncertain
Plans made get scattered and tossed
Life's focus shifts out of balance
And battles hard fought are lost

Bring out that bottle of the good stuff
We'll toss back a few in his name
Dear Mike, we're going to miss you
Without you it will never be the same

11

What can be said of life but that we live it? What can be said of death but that it takes from us what once lived?

⌒

Henry Gump Died Today

There are thoughts in my mind
Light as feathers
They float there
Elusive as feathers blown in the wind
They float there
But I can't catch them

I have memories
Memories of sun streaming through the window
Memories of happy singing and playing
Memories of the bobbing head, the flapping wings
Sometimes I imagine a flutter of breeze by my face
As of a tiny ghost flying by

Laying so still in your hand
So soft, so quiet, so innocent
A shudder of the green head
A stiffening of the legs
A curling of the feet
And then he was gone
Where do the tiny lives go?

I will remember him
I will remember all the others
All the others
Both the great and the small
They will never be far from my mind
They will float there
I will catch them

12

People love many things. They might love avocado salad or blackberry Jello with real whipped cream. They might love to dance or to gaze at a star filled sky. They love their spouses, their children, their parents, their family and their friends. And people love their pets.

People love being in love, giving love and getting love because love makes us happy. And that is why it also makes us sad when something we love has to go.

Our Good Boy

He probably left his yellow mark
In the morning snow
He probably trotted way out back
Where duty always called

Then he trotted homeward, nose in the air
His tail, a curved cane held high
To sit on the stoop, surveying his kingdom
With bright, intelligent eyes

Out of habit he probably trotted
Through the bush
To bark his one note song
Calling to a friend
He couldn't understand was gone

It only takes a second
It's odd how things can change
Normal is rear-ended
And things are not the same

Confusion bends the brain waves
The heart beat speeds and slows
Legs buckle and collapse
The breath catches in the throat

The last he felt, a gentle touch
Petting the side of his head
The last he heard, a high sweet voice
With words of praise and love

We'll always remember
The things he used to love
The things he used to do
Going for a walk
Staring down the squirrel

Having company
Asking for a treat
Running like a knucklehead
Sitting on your feet

Lying curled on his doggie bed
Surrounded by his toys
Our Dog Harley
Our good boy

13

Where would we be without memories? Good or bad, our pasts live there; defining our todays and guiding us as we head towards our tomorrows.

> 'The knife, all the memories, the sins he had committed. They were tearing Joe apart now. Because, of all the things that he had done since leaving Bizmark Street, the one thing he had never done was forgive himself.'
> Excerpt from 'License – A Novel'

Memories

Memories, like shadows
Sleepwalk deep within our minds
The past
For good or bad
Inhabiting their vague outlines

A sight, a sound, jogs them from their sleep
They become a pinprick of light
Dim hint of dawn on the horizon
Then spreading and morphing to bright

How things were!
Perhaps you smile
Who you knew!
Bittersweet
What you did!
Fond nostalgia
And what was done.
Buried terror, guilt, shame, defeat

The present calls you away from your reflection
Memories fade back to the shadowlands
Some leave you with a kiss
A smile upon your lips
Some leave you with trembling hands

14

There was a wedding and relatives closer than us to the bride and groom were not invited. One of the uninvited was devastated, hurt beyond measure that he had been excluded. And he could not understand why.

So I inquired on his behalf and was told there were deep seated issues, which they declined to elaborate on. The uninvited was dumbstruck. He had no idea that issues even existed.

All I could remember was the love I had seen pass between the two over the years. I couldn't help but think that a mistake was being made, one that would some day be regretted.

Satin Lined Box

Our time on this earth
Is too short to hold grudges
When the last breath is taken
That's the end

And you'll find yourself standing over
A satin lined box
Crying for the still figure
Cradled within

Crying for the years
Lost and wasted
Knowing too late
How foolish you've been

15

'"Greg!" Dixie screamed in panic, just as the machine monitoring his life forces began to emit a loud, steady beep, the squiggly lines running flat across the screen.

"Code Blue, Code Blue. Recovery 205. Code Blue, Code Blue, Recovery 205." Blared through the halls.'

Excerpt from 'License – A Novel'

Star

I have your folder full of songs
And I have your guitar
They were given to me by your family
When you became a star
Shining down from above

You sang those songs to me
Your voice so clear and true
Words of heartache, love and loss
Echoed around the room

You could have been a star
And now you really are
Shining down from above

Your voice remains in my head
Your words remain in my heart
Remain in the corners of my room
Covered with cobwebs and dust

If my heart ever heals
I'll pick them up
I'll wipe them off
With a soft velvet cloth

I'll toss them up to the sky
So you can catch them
They will hang by your side
Like faceted diamonds
Like colorful gems
Shining down from above

You could have been a star
And now you really are
Shining down from above

16

We all know that death is part of life. It's the inevitable ending that every living thing comes to on this earth.

But sometimes I wonder – What happens after someone dies? Where do they go? Do I believe in heaven? Do I believe in ghosts?

I've felt a flutter against my cheek when I was alone in the room and all the windows were closed. I've heard a whisper in my ear when no one else was there. At those times, I have to say the answer is yes.

"'Mike?" Dixie asked, suddenly serious, her blue/green eyes gazing across the table into Mike's eyes of grey, "Do you believe in ghosts?"'
Excerpt from 'License – A Novel'

Ghost

Gravity has no hold on me
   I float like a balloon
   Unhindered
   Softer than a whisper

But a whisper needs breath
And breath I have left behind

Higher and higher I float
　　Surrounded by calm, acceptance and serenity
　　Still, although up is where I go
　　Down is where I look
　　I see
　　But my living eyes are closed

Ones that I have loved
　　I see them on the ground
　　They look up as I look down
　　They wale inconsolable
　　So much grief, so much sorrow
　　I ache to comfort them
　　Try to tell them my soul is at peace and free
　　But words no longer belong to me

Still they weep
　　Time is what they need
　　Time will blend their heartache and sorrow
　　Into a new normalcy, a happy tomorrow
　　Burning tears and anguished sobs
　　Will be replaced by nostalgic memories
　　Whenever their thoughts turn to me

*T*ime passes differently here
    Minutes and smells
    Colors and days
    Music and shapes
    They all combine
    I float content
    And hope they know I watch over them
    In the twinkle of the stars
    In the warmth of the sun
    Love and life go on
    In more ways than one

17

Unhatched

The dog scared her up one day
Exploding from her hideout
Green brown head on out-stretched neck
Wings flapping
Webbed feet skimming the ground

She didn't go far
Not nearly as far as we did
High tailing it wide eyed
Hearts thumping
More scared than she

She kept her dark eye on us
Waited till we went inside
Then waddled back

And disappeared into the ground cover
While I kept my blue eye on her
Peeking from the window

Every day I glanced there
Nonchalant as I passed
As if I didn't know
Spotted the top of her smooth feathered head
Saw dappled sun glinting in her stone dark eye
Alert and statue still
Warming and protecting her secret

Her secret
At the base of the snowdrift crab
Hidden by pachysandra's glossy toothed leaves
Soft downy lined depression
Cradling and cushioning
A clutch of creamy white eggs

Expectant
We both waited
Patient mother-to-be and smiley faced I
For determined pecks
And broken shells
And peeping bundles of maize colored fluff

For weeks I glanced as I passed
Craning my neck for a yellow glimpse
To see only the gleam of her green brown head
My smiling anticipation turning to unease
And questions about duck eggs
Tapping out on the keys

Then one day she was gone
Instinct whispering in her ear
It has been too long
Fly now
Care for yourself
There will be nothing needing you here

There were only three of them in the nest
Eggs that never hatched
She had sat there all that time
Devoted and without complaint
All for naught
All in vain

And I wondered
If she had waddled away
Confused
Searching for what she had somehow missed
Lusterless now her dark eye
Aching loss in her feathered breast

I still glance there as I pass
Missing her green brown head
Missing her stone dark eye
Missing the furry feathered life
That never came

18

A nest is built as a safe place to protect and nurture the little
ones. A place where the little ones can learn the ways of
the world and grow until their wings are strong enough to fly.
And fly they must, because a nest is a temporary place, and little
ones are meant to grow up and leave it.

To Grow Away

A baby is born so precious and small
Unable to do a thing
Except cry when she is hungry
Or needing anything

You hold them to you closely
To love and protect with all your might
You know what you have to do
Prepare them for that distant someday
When they grow up and away from you

You teach them how to walk and talk
You teach them the colors and the shapes
Red and blue, round and square
And the sounds that the animals make

You teach them the difference
Between their elbows and their knees
And how to use the toilet
When they have to take a pee
Right from wrong, good from bad, weak from strong
How to share their toys
And how to get along

You teach them to respect and to obey
How to sort the laundry
How to fry an egg
How to save their money
For a rainy day
Because you know its nature's plan
For them to go away

And when that day arrives
As they're heading out the door
As you long to hold them closely
For just a little bit more
You'll know you've done your job
You've done what's right and true
You have taught them how
To grow away from you

19

'She knew Tony didn't understand how she could be home all day and not seem to get anything done. He got upset with her sometimes. But it's not like she could just leave Daisy and Bower to their own devises while she cleaned and straightened the house all day! Daisy was only five and Bower was still a toddler in diapers! She had to get them dressed and cleaned up, get them breakfast, lunch and snacks, entertain them and keep them happy and safe.'

Excerpt from 'License – A Novel'

Threads

Something round and something white
Bothers you both day and night
Pitter pat of little feet
Nothing ever seems to stay neat
Laughing, crying, tears and smiles
Love rolling around all the while

Threads intertwining, intermingling, getting tangled
Sometimes you think you're going to get strangled
Always the threads get straightened out
And words of love are the ones you want to shout

Something round and something white
The threads that kept it together weren't right
But now everything is all better
I re-sewed the button on your sweater!

20

'The soft nighttime light spilling through the curtains had a brightness to it tonight - moonlight reflecting off falling snow. Maybe she should go to the window and see how much snow had fallen? But why? There was no reason really. No reason to get out of the warm bed, to leave Boyd's side......'

Excerpt from 'License – A Novel'

Moonlight

Paint it pale yellow
Or silvery white
Paint it cobalt
Or dark midnight

Paint descending shimmers
In translucent creams
And blend them at the bottom
Into a nebulous dream

Add tinges of soft blues and grays
Paint a delicate hushed glow
Paint moonlight
Reflecting on snow

21

Sometimes the future has a way of sneaking up on us. We turn our heads and suddenly realize the future is here. Years have gone by! What have we done with them? Did we live those years the way we should have? Did we follow through with our intentions? How much have we accomplished? And how much time have we wasted?

'How many times had she rebuffed his tender advances, offered her cheek instead of her lips, turned her back on his smile, tuned out his recounting of his day or his discussions of things that mattered to him, too consumed by the bad seed to react or respond?'
Excerpt from 'License – A Novel'

Wasted

Clouds tinged pink and feathery
Decorate the azure sky
The sun's radiant fire
Reflected
In morning's golden eye

But I'm stuck behind a city bus
Stop go stop go stop go
Street cleaner in another direction
A constant state of slow

Plans of promise change
Amidst the glances and the stares
Warning me of staying
Preventing me from going anywhere

Young couples like bright suns on the sidewalk
So happy, so vital, so alive
Fragile future spread out before them
Their brightness brings tears to my eyes

But I had this once – this youth
And you!
Eyes held the mischievous gleam of the rogue
Hard lust often turned down and wasted
Why I don't even know

Love still sweet and tender
Warm memories
firm and velvety soft
Desire still burns hot and fierce
But abilities have become a little lost

Contents might shift on take off
A sideways glance draws attention away

I've seen enough furtive fingers fiddling
To know things need to be rearranged

Things lost and found connect somehow
Like colors on a wheel
Yellow and red swirl to orange
Yellow and blue to green

Vibrant leaves of yellow gold
Cover morning's pure white snow
Plans of promise wasted
Stop go stop go stop.....
Go

22

O f emptiness and depression. Of unhappiness and despair.

'Emma Baxter knew she wasn't perfect. She was sometimes quick tempered and quarrelsome. She let other people walk all over her. She had a tendency to daydream and was inclined to be overly thrifty. She didn't need Caleb to point these things out to her.

Why couldn't he point out her good qualities instead? Like that she was lively and energetic. That she was a good cook. That she was friendly, smart, reliable and helpful. That she told funny jokes.'

Excerpt from 'License – A Novel'

Broken

A brief smile
A yellow glimpse
So long since I've felt this way
Too soon it will all be departed

Driving down the road
Is it Spring now or
Winter that's on the way?

A thick fog is pushing me down
Like writer's block on life
Happiness is quickly erased
Your pencil
Draws disappointment and disgust
You have seen me naked
What can I hide?

23

When confronted by our failures, we often deny the charges, or make up excuses, or try to prove them wrong. We do not always succeed.

⌒

Steel

I am steel
Determined, cold and hard
And steely eyed
I stare you down

With time and moisture
Hard grey corrodes
to rusty red
And salty, moist tears
Rust my steely resolve

I am steel
Disintegrated and full of holes
Weak in the end
Not really strong

24

We tend to gravitate towards those that share our values and our outlook on life. We become friends with them, we fall in love with them.

But people are complex creatures and relationships are complex things. We cannot look at the world or the people that inhabit it through any eyes but our own. We can think we know someone, we can sympathize or empathize with them, but our perception is still colored by our own experiences, our own values, and the way we live our own lives.

And sometimes we find our perceptions about someone have been wrong. We thought that they were using the same bright yellow crayon that we were. But the crayon they are holding now is stormy gray.

Was it ever yellow? Did we ever really know them? Did they ever really know us? And for that matter, do we really even know ourselves?

Strangers

I don't understand your world
But know that neither do you understand mine
We sit seemingly together
But actually apart most of the time

I thought we were on the same wave length
Concepts and opinions hovering similar lines
Now it seems we've both been lying
Who are you?
Who am I?
Who's to blame?

Apologies if I've hurt you
It was love I meant to send
After all these years we're strangers
Everything lost
Nothing gained

And I've always wanted to say this
Though it will make no sense to you
You've always been
The better man
But I
Am not a man at all

25

'Greg strapped on the guitar and looked at Dixie. "Now, I want you to pretend like you don't know me, like you don't know about us." His voice was soft, almost a whisper. "Pretend I'm just some guy you never saw before in your whole life standing on a stage in some no name club or at a little hometown festival, singing some songs. Can you do that Dixie?"'

Excerpt from 'License – A Novel'

About You (Lyrics)

Elusive
Elusive song
Jumbled words float like feathers in the air

You said I should write about
Something that I know about
But the only thing I know about
Is you

I could write about the moon and stars above
I could write about the sun up in the sky
The sun as warm and bright as your face
The stars like sparkles in your eyes

I could write about walking on a summer's day
I walked with you, our fingers were entwined
I could write about morning grasses tipped with glistening dew
Dewy drops like tear drops if I made you cry

I could write about the time
A dog pissed on my shoe
But the dog was yours
And the song was really about you

You said I should write about
Something that I know about
But the only thing I know about
Is you

Read between the lines, you'll see
Every song's the same, you'll see
Every song is really about you

Everything I write about
The only thing I know about
Every song is really about you

Elusive
Elusive song
Jumbled words float like feathers in the air
The poet in my heart tries to catch them as they float there
The poet in my heart
Released by losing you

26

'The friendly wave and bit of conversation as they passed the white ranch on the corner of Burlwood and Dragonfly became a thing of the past, and their friendship with the Akermans drifted away, just as Brenda and Clay's relationship with each other left completely the realm of love and togetherness and vanished into nothingness.

How could love be lost? How could it disappear entirely from someone's heart? How could its vacant spot be claimed by indifference or even hate?

These were questions Lainey couldn't answer. In a language she didn't understand. And never planned to learn.'

Excerpt from 'License – A Novel'

Love's Loss

There must have been a reason
For the bended knee
The ring and the vows
There must have been that feeling of completeness
Eyes soft and glistening
Two hearts brimming over with love

Did they forget that first glimpse
How their eyes caught
How their hearts pounded in their chests
Did they forget the court and the spark
Did they forget what they gave each other
Both tender and fierce
Under the covers in the dark

Did they know their love was lost
Did they search for it
Did they fight to get it back
Did they struggle with the thief that stole it
And try to wrench it from his grasp

Or did they just sit, watching it fade
Waving goodbye
As it evaporated and floated away
Only realizing too late
The brutal tragedy
Of their mistake
And how much they would miss it
When love was gone

27

No relationship is perfect, because people aren't perfect. An annoying habit might eat into a bad mood. A misspoken word might rattle around and echo between the ears. And then - there's an argument.

◡

Imperfections

By rote we do these things now, you and I
Hands clasped
Side by side
The kiss hello
or goodbye

But the smile is lame on my face
Dead the light in my eyes
Tired my mouth
of shaping itself around useless words

'Imperfection' shouts out at me
From your judgmental stare
From the critical line of your mouth
From the sorry shake of your head

I forgot
Wrong word
Tripped on a crack
Skewed memory
Unobservant
Not enough salt
Too much wine
Too spineless
Too silly, too naïve

Every flaw
waves large at you
You examine them with a magnifying lens
You highlight them with a fluorescent pen
Your eyes blind
as ethereal perfection dances by

Unnoticed

In whispered confidences
A warm touch
Complete faith
The give and the take

A joyful hello
The notes in a song
A color streaked sky
In love's sparkling eye

And I cry
We bicker and argue
We continue by rote
Wretched
Zombie like survivors

Until we long for each other again
and you lose your magnifying lens
Until the reasons evaporate
and fade into mystery

Until
warm again
is our kiss
Trembling and tender
our touch
Perfect
our imperfections

28

Perfection. We search for it, as if it is a hidden thing. We long for it, as if it is unattainable. This is never more true than during the holidays.

But perfection has always been right in front of us. If it is hidden, it is only by our own blind eye.

⌐

The Perfect Christmas

I could paint you a perfect picture
A Rockwell sort of scene
The fireplace warmly glowing
The scent of pine drifting
And colored lights twinkling merrily on the tree

The presents would be opened
All eyes would open wide
As they saw the gifts of all their dreams
Appearing at their sides

Warm and savory smells would be wafting in the air
Luring us to the dinner table set with Christmassy care
Sparkling china and crystal goblets
Golden candles flickering
A hush would be upon us as you made a special toast
"Of good health, good luck and good fortune,
may we all be able to boast!"

But Uncle Rob has had too much to drink
And is snoring on the couch
The kids, soon bored with all their gifts,
Are starting now to pout
Grandma too is nodding off
And Grandpa's tongue is wagging
Where did all the spirit go?
Something seems to be lacking!

And over at another house
Don't think it's any grander
Your cousins, Molly and Ryan, are arguing
They couldn't be any madder
Little Owen is breaking all his toys
Sophia now is crying
Mike is leaving before dinner is served
And your sister Amelia is despairing

A gathering there will surely be
A Norman Rockwell scene
But more like a comedy movie
The feeling in the air will be

No place is perfect at Christmas
Only in a dream
But things really are not as dreadful
As they might at first seem

Ignore the arguing, ignore the tears
But hold on tight
To the laughter ringing in your ears
Hold tight to the gleam in a young child's eye
The smile on a loved one's face
The feeling of warmth spreading to your soul
As you are held in a friend's embrace

Open your eyes and you will see
Your heart and you will feel
The love you give and the love you get
It is a perfect Christmas after all!

29

The newspaper in my hometown had put out the call for community members to send in stories, memoirs, family histories, character studies and other true stories about living here - in Rochester, NY. Selected entries would become part of 'Story Walk', an interactive sidewalk to be built on the grounds of the Memorial Art Gallery.

Excited, I sent in several stories, but the poet in me could not resist. I also sent in one poem. The poem and one of my stories made it through to the final round of the selection process.

Here is the poem.

My Rochester, My Home

I've lived in Rochester all my life.

So many memories:

Starry night skies and crickets singing their starry night songs.

Juicy pink watermelon picnics with golden, toasty marshmallows hot and gooey on the end of a stick.

Huge piles of dry crunchy brown leaves burning at the curb.

Frozen icy ponds and frozen icy toes.

Racing my Daddy down the street – Who thought he'd win?

Riding the bus to work in my green waitress dress, white apron tight around my waist – off to the Sibley Luncheonette.

Kissing that brown-eyed boy in the high school halls, my heart going pitter pat.

And going pitter pat as I walked down the aisle, white dress flowing, to meet him.

Long city walks with the kids in the stroller

And searching for our lost cat – Jack O'Lantern, where are you?

As I live and breathe,

As I dance and sing,

As I laugh and cry,

As I love and am loved.

This is my Rochester.

This is my home.

30

Alas, my poem did not make it onto the Story Walk. But my story did! And on the chance that you'd like to see it, even though it is not a poem, here it is.

Zucchini Soup

My husband's grandmother had been quite the cook. Every Sunday as a young boy, he would go to her house on Hollister street with his Papa, dreaming of what wonderful smells and flavors would be waiting for him; maybe spaghetti sauce with just the right tomatoey tang, or plump, homemade ravioli, maybe Sfingi (spongy Italian doughnuts dipped in honey) or her sturdy Italian cakes with white lemony icing. His mouth would water with anticipation.

All those wonderful recipes were stored in her head, she had never written them down, and when Grandma passed, the recipes died with her.

Over the years, we tried to recreate those recipes with little luck. Getting the right combination of flour, eggs, sugar and baking powder for the baked goods proved a feat never to be accomplished and recipes gotten on line touting themselves as "the traditional Italian favorite" never met the mark. The savory items were a little easier to duplicate but never quite achieved the perfect title of "Like Grandma's".

There was one recipe though that did occasionally hit the jackpot and that was zucchini soup. Every year I make a big pot towards the end of summer. Some years I win, some years I lose.

The most important thing you have to start with is a huge zucchini; one that hid under the leaves and didn't get spotted until it was almost the size of a watermelon with a pithy center and seeds as big and hard as those you would dig out of a pumpkin at Halloween. The next most important thing is to make teeny, tiny meatballs to put in the soup. "Grandma could form and fry those little meatballs so fast!" my husband would tell me. Then you add water, tomatoes, potatoes, celery, onions, garlic, basil and spices.

One year I forgot the potatoes! One year I added pasta. "No, No! Grandma never put pasta in her soup!" One year I just fried up the hamburger and broke it up into small pieces instead of fussing with all those little meatballs. How much difference could it make? Big difference - Not like Grandma's!

I got the big kettle out again this year. I had the humongous zucchini. I had two jars of canned tomatoes from my father's garden. I made the teeny, tiny meatballs and I made sure I added potatoes. Will this be the year? Will it measure up?

I watched my husband's face closely as he bought the steaming spoon to his lips and tasted the soup. There was a full-face light up! His eyes gleamed and sparkled! His smile was wide! "Oh, this is good! Just like my Grandma's!"

Success.

31

*'There was nothing better after a hard day's work than to pop
the top on a nice cold one and sit on his patio relaxing in the shade.'*
Excerpt from 'License – A Novel'

A Glass Of Ale

A load of nails
A load of hail
A load of salt
A load of mail
And a glass of ale

Hard work
Hard weather
Hard sweat
Hard bills
And aaaaaah

32

Peeople live their lives, they follow their dreams, they fall in love, they make mistakes.

'She should have run into Greg's arms. She should have kissed his cheeks, his eyes, his lips.

But instead Dixie, foolish Dixie, went into the kitchen and started opening cupboards and running water.

She said, "I'll make tea."

Instead of, "I love you, Greg."

And later she said, "You must be tired. The couch is pretty comfortable. I've fallen asleep on it lots of times."

Instead of, "Stay with me tonight, Greg. Please. Stay."'

Excerpt from 'License – A Novel'

Torn

I feel torn in two by emotions
Not knowing which is true
And which is false

Diane Rivoli

I feel like two separate people
Both of them scrambling for answers
Both of them lost

One is yellow and green
Bright as a summer's day
One is gray and violet
Like clouds before the rain

Questions swirl and whirl
They bash into my heart
I know the answers I scramble for
But I will not let them out

Gray rain will fall like tears
Yellow sun bores through the sorrow
Coaxing, calling, foretelling
The bursting forth of flowers

Those flowers,
So bright the purple and the pink
So bright against the brown earth
Like jewels to pierce your soul

I must let the jewels pierce me
The answers I have hidden
Will flow out bright and red

To love or not to love?
Soul mate or weight to hold me down?
I know these answers
Why am I so afraid?

Answering
Will make my torn self
Whole again

33

'He smiled but only for a moment. All his smiles turned to frowns these days. All days were worthless days without Dixie. What good was anything without his Dixie?

Maybe he could write a song after all. Without. That's what he'd call it. Without.'

Excerpt from 'License – A Novel'

Without *(Lyrics)*

Had the morning started out
Any different from another?
Life's dreams, all shattered
Lay surrounding me and laughing
At my innocence and naivety

Morning sky opens pink
On a worthless day
All days are worthless days
Since you went away
I am without

Sun
Tries to bore a hole into my ice cold heart
Tries to push through the pain and the sorrow
Tries to bring a smile to my lips
If only for a little while

Worthless efforts
On a worthless day
I am without

Without happiness
Without purpose
Without love
Without you

Where is the hand to pull me from these depths?
My own hand has grown weak
Will no one come and rescue me?
Help me glue back the shards of my dreams

What is it that I said?
What is it that I didn't say?
What is it that I did
Or didn't do
That made you go away?

Now I am without you

34

'Dixie hadn't been aware, not on a conscious level, that this was the exact one year anniversary of that devastating weekend. But the knowledge of it must have been keeping time in the back of her mind because when she looked, sleepy eyed, out at the little patch of petunias across from her window, the purple and white striped ones had stood out, bolder and brighter than all the others. And she had known.'

Excerpt from 'License – A Novel'

September

And here it was, September,
and the air was warm and chill at the same time

Last year this day had been on a Friday
This year it was on a Saturday instead

At this time last year, on a Friday night,
he should have been playing to a packed house
at the Lyell Road Tavern or Stoney's

Instead he had come to sing to her

And he had stood right there, next to the couch,
with his guitar strapped over his shoulder
and his green t-shirt
and his tight jeans

With his hazel eyes
and crooked smile
and tousled sandy hair

And she had sat right there, on one of the dinette chairs,
listening to him sing
watching the emotions pour out and overtake his face
his voice laughing the words or crying them
cradling them or chewing them up and spitting them out
feeling those emotions pour then into her

And he had made her realize
that she still loved him

And she had let him leave anyway

And the next morning.....
How could it possibly be true?

She had rushed to the hospital

He had been so weak
his skin so pale
almost as colorless as the white sheets on bed
as colorless as the white walls

But he had still smiled at her,
and he had squeezed her hand

And then …..

And he used to dye his hair purple
And he used to play in a band
And he used to wink at her in the crowd

He used to snort sometimes when he laughed
And eat his French fries with gravy
And guzzle his beer

And he used to run his hands so slowly down her body
and kiss her so tenderly that she swooned

But that was before

Before that day last September

Not now

Not anymore

35

A book comes to an end. A movie comes to an end. But really there is no end. There's always tomorrow. The story continues. Life goes on.

A Blank Page And A Pen

Spring pink leaves
Glow in the spotlight
Of the sun's last refracting rays
The sky explodes with color
At the end of the day

White starry jasmine
Honeys the emerging night
Scent set free
And drifting
In day's fading light

A page is turned
Night's dark curtain falls
Moon and stars
Embroidered
In shades of white and gold

Day will come again
A blank page
Waiting for a pen
And ever changing colors
To fill the hours in

Day to night
Night to day
A blank page and a pen
Lives may fade
Circumstances change
But the story never ends

36

Poems can be deep and full of meaning. But sometimes, they're light and fluffy things, done just for fun; still full of meaning never-the-less.

I wrote this poem for my husband, my greatest inspiration and the love of my life, on his fifty-sixth birthday.

⟜⟶

1956

1956 was the year
That Elvis first hit the charts
Heartbreak Hotel was the song
The Wizard of Oz first appeared on TV
And "To Tell the Truth" came along

Eisenhower was President
Marilyn married husband number three
Martin and Lewis did their last act together
And the snooze alarm was invented by GE

A gallon of gas was 22 cents
For two thousand you could buy a new car
"The Edge of Night" was introduced
And Charlton Heston and Grace Kelly were big stars

Mel Gibson, Tom Hanks
And Carrie Fisher were all born in that year
Chris Isaak and David Copperfield were too
But the BIGGEST star born that year
Was wonderful, incredible YOU!!

Now, perhaps you haven't noticed
Or thought about it much
But there seems to be some
Significance
To your birthday this year (2012)

The year you were born – 1956
Your age – 56
56 might be a key
A chance at something spectacular
Like winning the lottery!

If you chew your food 56 times before you swallow
Or brush your hair for 56 strokes
Maybe something wonderful might happen
Nah, that would just be like some silly joke

Maybe if you drink 56 different kinds of beer
Now that would be a fun thing to try
Or go to 56 different restaurants
To judge which one has the best fish fry

No matter what your 56th year does bring
No matter what the ups or the downs
You really do have a key
A very special key
You've had it right from the start
You have the key to my new pair of roller skates
You have the key to my heart

And what better place to land than here, with a song in our
hearts,
floating on light and fluffy notes
of love.

Every Moment is a Poem
Every Poem a Song

The End

Author's Musings

When I first began compiling the poems for *Every Moment is a Poem, Every Poem a Song,* this thought kept coming to my mind – Exactly what is the definition of a poem? And more specifically, I wondered - Would the definition include the word 'rhyme'?

And so, of course, I looked it up.

<u>Online Dictionary</u>
POEM
po·em
noun
- A piece of writing that partakes of the nature of both speech and song that is nearly always rhythmical, usually metaphorical, and often exhibits such formal elements as meter, rhyme, and stanzaic structure.
- Something that arouses strong emotions because of its beauty.

I was curious about this rhyme thing because, when I was first introduced to poetry as a child, I was taught that poems should rhyme; that rhyming was the defining reason for their existence.

It might be because of this that I am prejudiced towards poems that rhyme. They are usually my favorites, both to read and to write. But the fact is that many poems are not written in verse, some of my own poems included.

So then I wondered – What do other people think of when they hear the word 'poem'? Do they think of rhyming words? What would people say if they were asked to give, in their own words, the definition of a poem?

And so, of course, I asked them.

What Is A Poem?

<u>Amy R.</u>
– A poem is a glimpse into a person: their experiences, their aspirations, their fears, their imagination, their journey.

<u>Matt H.</u>
– A poem to me is a piece of writing that I can relate to emotionally. It has feeling, it has emotions, it has substance.

<u>Lisa B.</u>
– Feelings from the heart.

<u>Josh R.</u>
– Poetry can be abstract phrases used to express something that cannot be expressed in literal words. Or it can be metaphors that

illustrate a point more clearly than the actual subject matter. It can be phrases set in a pattern that makes it more artful. Even completely literal phrases written in normal prose can be so well crafted that it could be considered poetry. Any of these types of poetry can be combined. And they can all be made to rhyme if the writer chooses.

Joe R.
– Words that sometimes rhyme and that usually don't make sense.

I had been hoping for an avalanche of responses. Instead my inbox was graced with only a smidgen. Of the few that I did receive, less than half of them used the word 'rhyme' to define a poem.

What does this prove?

In survey land, this would be akin to conducting a poll using an equation with a coefficient of zero, the arrived at results yielding a zero percent accuracy rate.

It proves nothing to the community at large.

To me it proves that poems are poems – imaginative, emotional, heartfelt, artful, individual and unique. And that, whether they rhyme or not, makes no difference at all.

About the Author

D iane Rivoli lives in beautiful upstate New York with her husband of 40 plus years, Joseph. She enjoys the changing of the seasons, singing karaoke, puttering in the garden, partaking of fine wines and entertaining family and friends. She also greatly enjoys visits to the now empty nest by the two grown sons that vacated years ago and the daughter-in-law of her dreams.

She finds inspiration in memories of the past and thoughts of the future, in the smiles that dance in the eyes of those she loves or in the tears that might pool there, in the drops of rain that cling to the window screen or the determined leaf that clings alone to a winter bare tree, in a harsh word, in a wagging tail, in simply being alive.

In addition to her poetry book, *Every Moment is a Poem, Every Poem a Song,* Diane is also the author of *License,* a novel about people living their lives, following their dreams, falling in love and making mistakes.

www.dianerivoli.com

dianerivoli@yahoo.com

Made in the USA
Middletown, DE
30 December 2016